CONTENTS

Introduction

One of the newest of the developed nations, Australia sits on the most ancient of land-masses, its brilliant, glittering, high-rise cities circling a vast wilderness of desert and a harsh outback. Visitors cannot fail to be amazed by its contrasts. Cosmopolitan urban centres like Sydney and Melbourne offer a level of culture and sophistication to rival any city, yet they are within hours of gorgeous golden beaches and spectacular mountain scenery. And if you venture farther from the city, you discover an almost mystical land of beautiful colours, surreal rock formations and untouched rainforests.

Australians are blessed with almost three million square miles of land, and with only 16 million of them to share it, that leaves a lot of space. It is no surprise, then, that given these natural advantages Australians cherish an outdoor lifestyle which makes the most of their glorious climate. From water sports and "barbies" to Aussie Rules, cricket and rugby, the popular images of Australia portray a healthy, energetic, fun-loving people at ease with themselves and their environment. Sometimes called "the lucky country", Australia seems almost blissfully isolated from the turmoil of the twentieth century. But it has had its share of trials and tribulations, its winners and losers, and it was only out of considerable suffering, courage and hard work that the modern Australia was born.

When Captain James Cook landed at Botany Bay in 1770, Australia was a little-known continent as far away from Britain as any place could be. Portuguese and Dutch explorers had charted much of the coastline while looking for gold and spices, but virtually nothing was known of the interior, and the first settlers to land in Sydney Cove in 1788 were not even sure if the known parts added up to a continuous landmass. To this motley assortment of convicts, sailors and petty officials the great natural beauty of this remarkable continent must have seemed inhospitable and utterly alien. Six months away from Britain and without any real hope of return, the first convicts who were transported (often for as little as the theft of a loaf of bread) must have despaired of their situation. But the almost immediate influx of free settlers led to the rapid exploitation of the interior and a steady growth in the colony.

This exploitation was not without its price. The forested uplands and plains that the vigorous British were rapidly colonising were not uninhabited, and as with the Native Americans 150 years earlier, a combination of European disease, drink and land hunger devastated the Aboriginal population of the fledgeling New South Wales. To a migratory people who thought the land sacred, investing individual features of the landscape with the spiritual identities of their forebears, the legalistic and proprietorial British attitude was incomprehensible. In the ensuing clash of interests and cultures, the Aborigines were the inevitable losers and their lifestyle was almost eradicated by the white settlers.

The exploitation of this new and exciting land continued nevertheless, and by the 1830s and 1840s bold individuals were settling along the fertile coastal plain and discovering new opportunities beyond an unbroken chain of forbidding mountains. Naturally, in such a land, the rugged explorer has an important place in its folklore. Famous expeditions, such as Sturt's down the Murrumbidgee and Murray rivers in 1829–30, helped to open up the south-eastern hinterland beyond the mountains of the Great Dividing Range, and Edward Eyre's epic journey across the waterless Nullarbor Plain to reach Albany in 1840–41 was equally heroic.

However, it was a geological rather than a geographical discovery that really lit the touch-paper of Australian development. In 1851, gold was found in Bathurst, New South Wales, and then in Ballarat and Bendigo in Victoria. The ensuing gold rush sparked a 40-year boom and saw the flowering of magnificent buildings in Melbourne and Sydney, as well as in the gold towns themselves. Indeed, the year 1851 has particular significance for all Australians, for this was also the year in which the city of Melbourne broke away from New South Wales to begin its evolution into the premier commercial and industrial centre of Australia.

As the nineteenth century drew to a close, the newly confident Australian people thought the time was right for greater independence. A federal commonwealth of self-governing states with a degree of autonomy from Britain was the result, and on the first day of the new century the Commonwealth of Australia formally came into being. Until the end of World War II, the rapidly emerging modern state was still largely dependent on the mother country for its trade, finance and defence. Wool, wheat, meat and minerals were exported to Britain in exchange for manufactured goods, capital and a steady supply of immigrants.

But the relationship has always been far more than merely commercial, and ties of kinship and culture led thousands of Australians to fight in both world wars, in which they made distinguished contributions to the Allied war efforts. Since 1945, increasing numbers of immigrants, particularly from southern Europe and South-East Asia, combined with Britain's increasing inability to soak up Australia's exports, have forced the maturing nation to turn to its Asian neighbours. And today, it is Japan rather than Britain that is Australia's largest export market.

As Australia approaches the new millennium with thoughts of becoming a republic, the rapidly changing political and economic world presents many new challenges. But if the rugged individualism of Australia's past is anything to go by, few can doubt that it has the people and resources to meet these challenges with confidence.

Natural Wonders

This vast island continent was once part of an even larger landmass called Gondwanaland, which also comprised Africa, South America, Antarctica and India, but Australia lost contact with Antarctica 40 million years ago and was separated from the rest well before then. This isolation led to a very distinctive pattern of evolution, and much of Australia's beautiful and varied flora and fauna are unique.

Ever-present eucalypti, like the massive mountain ash of Victoria and Western Australia's karri, are found all over Australia, from the lush tropical rainforest in northern Queensland to the low lying "mallee" of the outback. The verdant rainforest of Tasmania, with its Huon pine and southern beech, is one of the world's last temperate wildernesses, while acacias, banksias and vibrant wild flowers can be found all over the continent. This distinctive landscape is shared by equally colourful and unusual beasts, from kangaroos and kookaburras to lizards and lorikeets.

The bulk of Western Australia, South Australia and the Northern Territory consists of dry plains and flat-topped plateaux – a seemingly endless wilderness of desert and scrubland broken only by low mountain ranges such as the Flinders and MacDonnell, and mysterious rock formations like the Olgas and Ayers Rock.

This "red centre" is an arid place where rain may not fall at all in some years, but the striking colours that transmute with the passing of the day – crimsons and violets, ochres and oranges – create amazing vistas which overwhelm you with their violent beauty and sheer size. Only around the edges, in the extreme south-west and the tropical north, is the rainfall high enough to support farmland and forest.

Move east into Queensland and New South Wales, and the desert gradually yields its grip to the bush and grassland of the outback. Most of this land is still only fit for cattle or sheep, but where rainfall permits, plains of wheat are common, and in the foothills and valleys farther south and east vineyards and attractive farms are found.

Farther east still are the spectacular cliffs, canyons and forests of the Great Dividing Range, which extends from Cape York to Tasmania. The range includes the stunning Blue Mountains, which proved such an obstacle to the early settlers, and the Snowy Mountains, which contain Australia's highest peak, Mount Kosciusko, as well as glacial lakes, forests of snow gums, and alpine heaths strewn with wild flowers.

The fertile coastal plain which runs around the eastern rim of the country forms an often stunning seascape. Wonderful sandy coves and rocky inlets run for over 2000 miles, from the dramatic headlands and stacks of the Twelve Apostles in Victoria, to the glorious string of tropical beaches and coral reefs that stretch along the Queensland coast. The natural wonders of Australia are surely unsurpassed.

PAGE 7: A spectacular view of one of the many waterfalls that cascade over the sandstone cliffs found in Morton National Park, part of New South Wales's Southern Highlands – an area popular with both tourists and the inhabitants of Sydney.

ABOVE LEFT: A panoramic view across the rugged heartland of the Blue Mountains in New South Wales. In the foreground are the sandstone pillars known as the Three Sisters.

LEFT: These limestone rock stacks, known as the Twelve Apostles, rise out of the waters of the Bass Strait and are to be found in Victoria's Port Campbell National Park, 100 miles south-west of Melbourne.

ABOVE: One of the country's greatest natural wonders is the curious Wave Rock found in Western Australia. It is more than 100 yards long and up to 16 yards high. Vertical stripes help to give the impression of a wave about to break onshore.

ABOVE: One of Western Australia's more unusual landscapes is to be found in the Nambung National Park, 150 miles north of Perth. Thousands of these weathered limestone pillars, known as the Pinnacles, are found in the park.

ABOVE RIGHT: A bush baby photographed at night. These diminutive nocturnal primates live in small groups and feed on insects, fruit and leaves. They are famous for their acrobatic tree climbing.

RIGHT: Ayers Rock – Uluru to the Aborigines – is undoubtedly the most famous of Australia's natural wonders. The red monolith was formed some 500–600 million years ago and reaches a height of well over 1000 feet.

LEFT: A pair of majestic gum-trees, a common sight in much of Australia. These two examples are to be found near Alice Springs.

ABOVE: The kookaburra, also known as the laughing jackass due to its distinctive call, is a type of kingfisher and feeds, in part, on reptiles.

ABOVE LEFT: Magnetic Island lies just off the coast from Townsville in Queensland. Access is by helicopter or ferry from the mainland.

LEFT: The Great Barrier Reef stretches some 1250 miles along the east coast. This view is from Cook's Lookout on Lizard Island.

ABOVE: The lush foliage of an Australian rainforest. This is Queensland's Fraser Island, the largest sand island in the world.

The Cities

With their steel towers and glass skyscrapers rising from the earth like enormous monuments to modernity, the bright new cities of Australia combine nature and structure in a most pleasing manner. All the major cities, with the exception of Canberra, are on the sea or near river mouths, and their unique juxtaposition of beaches, buildings and parkland create a healthy and vigorous environment that is hard to find elsewhere. The big cities certainly have their individual identities, yet they all combine the advantages of modern high-tech living with sunshine and scenery.

Of course, few skylines are more familiar than Sydney Harbour, with its Opera House, Bridge and Centrepoint Tower. But this vibrant, sprawling metropolis also has some wonderful parkland along the Harbour's 150-mile waterfront and still has remnants of its early convict origins at the Rocks, the site of the first European settlement.

This former den of vice is all a far cry from the carefully planned and beautifully manicured national capital of Canberra. Founded in 1911 on a geometrical plan, Canberra may lack the hustle and bustle of Sydney, but its fine mountain scenery and the spaciousness of its lakeside setting have their own appeal.

Sydney's great rival Melbourne once had a rather conservative and dull reputation, but the influx of immigrants from all over the world, especially southern Europe, and the redevelopment of much of the city centre has given rise to a cosmopolitan and civilised place which combines the best of nineteenth- and twentieth-century architecture.

Adelaide is a city of straight streets and spacious parks. Famed for its good food and biennial arts festival, this is an elegant and compact city within an hour of fine beaches, the beautiful Adelaide hills and the famous Barossa Valley wine country.

The fastest-growing and newest of Australia's big cities is also the most remote. But Perth not only has a setting of incomparable beauty on the banks of the Swan River, it is also the capital of a state with immensely rich mineral deposits – not surprisingly, it is sometimes called "the lucky city".

Relaxed, sunbaked Brisbane is also blessed in its proximity to natural beauty. To the south is the high-rise glitz of the Gold Coast and Surfers Paradise, and to the north is the magnificent Sunshine Coast. The famed rugged provincialism of its inhabitants may have mellowed, but this tropical city still has its own distinct character.

Hobart enjoys some historic colonial buildings and a beautiful setting on the Derwent estuary under the gaze of Mount Wellington, and Australia's rich gold-mining history has also produced some distinguished old towns. Bathurst, Bendigo, Ballarat and Kalgoorlie all rose from gold, and their fine buildings serve as a monument to Australia's past just as the gleaming towers of the big cities reflect Australia's present.

PAGE 17: Sydney Harbour Bridge pictured at night. Built on granite pillars, the bridge spans the waters separating Dawes Point and Mission Point. It was opened in 1932.

ABOVE LEFT: Sydney Harbour Bridge and Opera House at twilight. The distinctive Opera House, built on Bennelong Point, was the brainchild of Danish architect Joern Utzon and was completed in the early 1970s.

LEFT: The roofs of the Opera House, sometimes compared to shells or nuns' head-dresses, are covered by a million tiles. Inside, as well as the opera auditorium, there is a concert hall, cinema and library.

ABOVE: The beautifully preserved Vaucluse House is near the shores of Port Jackson at the mouth of Sydney Harbour.

LEFT: The Rocks, in Sydney, can be found near Dawes Point and were the site of the country's first European settlement. It once had a reputation for lawlessness in the early years of its occupation, but careful development and preservation has made the area one of the city's main attractions.

ABOVE: Flags billow over Canberra's Commonwealth Avenue. In the distance is Capital Hill, the site of the nation's new parliament building, which was opened in time for Australia's bicentennial celebrations in 1988.

ABOVE: Situated by the Yarra River, the Victorian Arts Centre is a complex of modern buildings. This spire adorns the Theatres building.

ABOVE RIGHT: Melbourne's memorial to Anzac troops, known as the Shrine of Remembrance, was based on the Parthenon in Athens.

RIGHT: The Melbourne skyline, photographed at night, provides a stunning backdrop to the Yarra River in the foreground.

23

CUSTOM HOUSE

ABOVE: Launceston Customs House, a reminder of Tasmania's close link with the sea, has been beautifully restored. It is just one of many Georgian and Victorian buildings in this city on the beautiful Tamar River.

RIGHT: The bustling Rundle Mall can be found in Adelaide, Australia's fifth-largest city. Adelaide's geometrical city plan was the brainchild of South Australia's Surveyor-General, Colonel William Light, in the 1830s.

LEFT: A view of Perth's Hay Street Mall. The city, Western Australia's state capital, combines stately buildings, both old and new, and a beautiful natural landscape.

ABOVE: The skyline of Perth reflects the city's new-found confidence, with tall office blocks nestling comfortably side by side with older buildings.

ABOVE: A vision of Perth's future. Reflected in the mirror-like windows of a sparkling skyscraper are the images of other office blocks.

RIGHT: Brisbane's Victorian General Post Office is dwarfed by the high-rise developments of Australia's third-largest city.

The People

The fact that the first Australians were forcibly deported and subjected to an oppressive regime by their own countrymen has obvious significance for the attitudes and outlook of modern Australians. The suffering and hardship endured in the penal colonies created bonds of comradeship and a distaste for the British establishment that are still evident today. Egalitarianism and a healthy disrespect for privilege and pretension (especially of the upper-class British variety) were the natural consequences of such origins and have become universally recognised Australian traits, even though most retain an affection for the mother country itself.

Unfortunately, until relatively recently this inherent sense of equality rarely extended to Aborigines, Asians or women, and few would deny that the development of Australia was sometimes accompanied by unsavoury and regrettable episodes, particularly white Australia's treatment of the Aboriginal population. But despite the problems that still exist, over the last few decades remarkable changes have been made.

In an age of increasing environmental awareness, Australians have begun to understand the lifestyle and thinking of the Aborigines. Their more sympathetic, and sustainable, relationship with the land is now something to be admired rather than derided. The "White Australia" policy is also a thing of the past, and high levels of immigration from South-East Asia have created a genuinely multicultural society. Even Australia's famous "manly" image is on the wane as the historically important ideals of rugged individualism are confronted with the reality of modern urban life.

Thankfully, one aspect of Australian society that shows no sign of undergoing a radical change is the fun-loving, open-air lifestyle. Whether surfing, sailing or swimming off magnificent beaches; bush-walking in the mountains or the outback; having a beer and a "barbie" in the garden; or simply soaking up the sun and lazing around in the great outdoors, Australians certainly know how to enjoy themselves.

There is no better place to see Australians really enjoying themselves than at a big sporting event. Sitting on "The Hill" at the Sydney Cricket Ground, or in a 120,000 crowd at the MCG for an Australian Rules final would give you the picture. But for the all-in package of sport, style and the chance to win a few dollars, the Melbourne Cup, Australia's premier horse race, takes some beating.

Of course, whether in the city or the outback, life is rarely all fun and games, and for the sheep farmer, miner or factory worker it is usually hot, hard work. In a nation which carved its existence out of an often inhospitable land, graft and persistence still have their place. But while recognising the value of hard work, no true Australian could ever become too obsessed by it — life is too short and the beach is too near for that.

PAGE 31: One of the key dates in Australia's national calendar is Australia Day, which is held on 26 January. Here, fireworks light up the night sky over Sydney.

ABOVE: Taking to the water in Sydney Harbour in celebration of Australia Day. Tall ships are surrounded by their smaller cousins, turning the Harbour into a hive of activity.

RIGHT: Doyle's On the Beach restaurant in Sydney is one of the most famous fish restaurants in the world. It can take up to 700 customers at a time and offers a superb view of the Harbour.

LEFT: Sheep farming remains one of the cornerstones of the Australian economy. Here, a New South Wales farmer separates a sheep from the rest of its flock.

ABOVE: Australian Rules football, a game based on Gaelic football which developed in Australia's gold fields, is one of the country's most popular sports. Up to 120,000 fans cram into the Melbourne Cricket Ground every September to watch the final.

ABOVE: Australia's wide-open spaces are captured in this shot of the Eyre Highway, a great looping route running from South Australia's Port Augusta across the Nullarbor Plain to Western Australia.

ABOVE RIGHT: Transporting camels in Western Australia. Camels that escaped from expeditions into the interior bred successfully and are now found in large numbers.

RIGHT: Life-savers are put through their paces on the golden beaches of Western Australia.

ABOVE: Tasmania's Port Arthur penal settlement, a testament to the harsh regime endured by early convicts, was begun in 1830.

ABOVE RIGHT: Time for a chat and a cooling drink in an Alice Springs bar. The pub is an important social focus in the outback.

RIGHT: The Old Telegraph Station at Alice Springs was part of the communications system between Adelaide and Darwin.

ABOVE: An Aboriginal child in the Northern Territories. After decades of exploitation, Aborigines are slowly regaining some of their lost rights.

ABOVE RIGHT: Advertising a pineapple farm in Queensland. This is the famous Sunshine plantation at Nambour.

RIGHT: A Beach Patrol jeep on the beautiful sands of Queensland's Surfers Paradise, the most famous resort on the Gold Coast.

LEFT: The seafront at Surfers Paradise comprises elegant shopping malls, the famed Cascade Gardens and several casinos. Elsewhere on Queensland's Gold Coast the atmosphere is quieter.

ABOVE: Townsville, Queensland, is Australia's largest tropical town and an ideal base for visiting the Great Barrier Reef. A university town, Townsville is also renowned for its late nineteenth-century botanical gardens and buildings dating from the same period.

OVERLEAF: "Beware of the Kangaroos". This vivid road sign in Queensland leaves you in no doubt as to its purpose.